Poetic Feelings

Poetic Feelings

C L Jones

Columbus, Ohio

This book is a work of fiction. The names, characters and events in this book are the products of the author's imagination or are used fictitiously. Any similarity to real persons living or dead is coincidental and not intended by the author.

The views and opinions expressed in this book are solely those of the author and do not reflect the views or opinions of Gatekeeper Press. Gatekeeper Press is not to be held responsible for and expressly disclaims responsibility of the content herein.

Poetic Feelings
Published by Gatekeeper Press
2167 Stringtown Rd, Suite 109
Columbus, OH 43123-2989
www.GatekeeperPress.com

Copyright © 2021 by C L Jones
All rights reserved. Neither this book, nor any parts within it may be sold or reproduced in any form or by any electronic or mechanical means, including information storage and retrieval systems, without permission in writing from the author. The only exception is by a reviewer, who may quote short excerpts in a review.

The cover design, interior formatting, typesetting, and editorial work for this book are entirely the product of the author. Gatekeeper Press did not participate in and is not responsible for any aspect of these elements.

Library of Congress Control Number: 2021940570

ISBN (paperback): 9781662914843
eISBN: 9781662914850

Contents

Reflection 1: Poetic Feelings   7
Poetic Feelings   9
Imagination   10
Blue   11
Where Does Love Begin?   12
Myself the Poet   13
Choice is but a Dream   14
I Can Remember   15
The Bench   16
A Tale of Two Lives   17
Teenage Beauty   18
Simply Living   19
Love at First Sight   20
Love at First Sight Cont.   21
Kidnapped   22
Beyond Not Seeing   23

Reflection 2: Poetic Interlude   25
Gamble   27
For Your Sake   28
Shoulder   29
Seven Days   30
Cheater   32
Lost   33
Bouncing Ball   34
A Jolly Soul Mate   35
Dear Friend   36
Together Only in Love   37
Runaway Love   38
Memory   39
Choices   40
Love Poem   41
Half Past   42

Reflection 3: Poetic Reckoning — 43
Could You — 45
Black America — 46
Suicidal Me — 48
World Gone Crazy — 49
I Am No More — 50
Don't Judge Me — 51
Trading Places — 53
Resistance/Existence — 55
Hand to Hand — 57
Take Me, Africa — 60
Young Guns — 61

Reflection 4: Poetic Fortitude — 63
Mother, May I? — 65
Note: I Slipped — 67
Carry on, Sisters — 68
Shoulder — 69
It Ain't Easy — 70
My Dues — 71
Cleanse Me — 72
My Birth — 73
One of Us — 74
In His Hands — 75
Sistergirl — 76
Any Other Road — 77
95 — 78

About the Author — 81
My Dedication — 83

Reflection 1:
Poetic Feelings

Poetic Feelings

I am only a young girl wanting to write poems
Of love, freedom, and broken-down homes
I want to write about the things that I feel,
Love and anger, the things that are real
I want to write about the things I lack
Of being proud of being black
The life and the culture that I am living
The people in the world that just stop giving

The person that was loved and is now left with pain
The thumps on my window that sound like rain
The clouds that seem to journey up above
The child that needs a mother, the child that looks for love

The darkness in the street and the death that passes away
The fear of waking up to a dark and gloomy day
The people in the street that form into a crowd
The poetic feelings that I dare not speak out loud
About life in particular, all I dare to be
The essence of life, the essence of me

Imagination

In my imagination, there is a world of peace
War has been forgotten, long-ago deceased
In my imagination, there is a sun that shines
Life is bright and wonderful; no one man is blind
In my imagination, there is a love that is true
Words are spoken poetically under a sky of blue
In my imagination, there is a world that cares
There are no burdens that, together, we cannot bear

Blue

What is blue?

Blue is the way I feel inside
When love is lost amidst the tide
Blue is the sound of a whistle scare
Damp and dark, arrested in air

Blues

What are the blues?

Sad lyrics to a sweet melody
Words that try to cry for me
The blues are a sudden reminder
That life was once much kinder
The blues so often lend
The harsh, bitter truth to a friend

Where Does Love Begin?

Where does love begin?
On what day does it end?

Does it start in a young one's heart?
Will it stay forever or drift apart?

Does it come with the rain?
Does it seep through a windowpane?

Does a bird drop it from above?
Where does it begin, this thing called love?

Does it stop in the sky and journey on again?
Where does it rest? Where does it end?

Does anyone know what it means?
Does it start when a lovebird sings?

Does anyone know where it began?
Does it rest a lady and tire a man?

Does it come from outside or live within?
Does anyone know where love begins?

Myself the Poet

A small room surrounded by books

An old manual typewriter, a cardboard file cabinet, and two unfinished books

I spent many days trying to convince the poet inside that the poet outside must write

I walked around with poems written on my jeans when there was nothing else to splatter my ink upon
My chalk-written words lined the cracked sidewalks above the hopscotch board on my street
I wrote on napkins, matchbooks, and even my skin. I wrote on everything that would accept my ink

People laughed at me and the things I chose to write on
But I still wrote
For the poet must write,
As the dreamer must dream

Choice is but a Dream

People do not accept me because I do not live straight their way
They say I am the epitome of sin because my heart is gay
Some people believe that I chose this life to live to the extreme
If they only knew that I have no control. That choice is but a dream

For years I lived in a closet; I lived my life a lie
I smiled while in your presence, when alone I cried and died
I spent my young life searching for strength and self-control
Only to discover that being gay was embedded in my soul

Still, I kept my feelings in a box for fear my friends would scatter
I hid my feelings from my family; acceptance was all that mattered
I have reached a point in my life; I am ready to take control
I am standing up for who I am, a living, breathing soul

I am stepping up to the challenge; I am facing my greatest task
I am standing up for who I am; I am taking off my mask
I can change the color of my hair; I can change my size, my weight
The one thing that I cannot change is the fact that I am not straight

I did not ask to be here, nor did I lose my way
I was born with an open mind, and I happen to be gay

Dedicated to the following warriors:
K Jones, G Douglas, F Sill, Ms. Nicolari

I Can Remember

When I hear your name
I imagine willows whispering in the wind
I can remember being a child,
Father, once again

I can see yesterday in shadows
Dancing before me
Faintly though brilliantly
I can remember being three

I can remember Fridays and Sundays
From beginning until end
I was six years old
When I asked you to be my friend

When the night falls upon me
When the wind is blowing wild
Somehow, Father,
I can remember being a child

The Bench

In a town not far from here
There sits a wooden bench
The planks I shellacked with my tears
Support the armrests that I clenched

I visited the bench for forty-nine days
It never weakened with my weight
Never questioned the length of my stay
Or the destiny of my fate

The golden-brown plywood slacks
Held me when I could not move
They kept my world intact
While my heart filled its splintered grooves

It was there that I told my story
It was there that I cried my tears
It was there that I found some solitude
On the bench I faced my fears

In a town not far from here
There sits a wooden bench
It gave my tears a place to land
My heart an arm to clench

A Tale of Two Lives

Who wins
Who loses
This battle
This war?
The young life
The old life
Is one life worth more?
Where do I fit into
This picture
This tale
A test filled with anguish
If I pass,
Have I failed?

The path has been cluttered
With reality and lies
Fear echoes the truth
When it escapes through the eyes
My heart's tugging reminds me
I am not always strong
While my mind leads me
To right what is wrong
My soul holds a secret
That stirs deep within
A tale of two lives
That death waded in

Teenage Beauty

Teenage beauty, I have tried
In the depths of sorrow, I have cried
I reached to touch your inner thoughts
At times of trial, we have fought

In a search of hope to bring you back
In a losing battle, your soul retracted
I strove to pull you from the ledge
My teenage beauty leaned toward the edge

I tried to love your every knack
I tried so hard to bring you back
Life had vanished from your face
Robbed its beauty and stolen its grace

I saw the blood; it dripped so fast
Through tears and sobs, I saw the past
My teenage beauty was reaching out to me
In the time of her need, I could not see

Teenage beauty, oh how I tried
In the depths of sorrow, I have cried

Simply Living

Walk over to the poor man sleeping on the park bench
Step into his worn-down shoes
Just for the moment
I ask you to feel for him, not because he is poor
Just because he is simply living

Walk with me through the alley on a cold winter night
Sit down next to the homeless woman
Slip into her ragged coat just for the minute
When the chill has run through the feeble cloth
Only then shall I ask you to feel for her, not because she is cold, but
Because she has chosen instead of easy dying to go on simply living

Walk with me through the suburbs of slums
Stand beside the orphaned child
As he searches through boxes of rotten food behind the grocery store,
Sit down on the curb and have dinner with him tonight
When you have devoured the last of the meal's flavors
I shall ask you once again to feel
Feel for him

Not because he is starving
Just because the abandoned, homeless, starving being has chosen
Through it all to go on.
Dying is easy;
The hard part is simply living
For the moment, by the minute, against the hour

Love at First Sight

Do I believe in love at first sight?
Falling in love beneath the moonlight
Passions burning out of control
Pitter-patter inside the soul

Do I believe in love at first sight?
Carelessly loving in broad daylight
Eating away at the body with lust
Handing over a heart with trust

Do I believe in love at first sight?
Souls embracing in the middle of the night
Tender kisses on wanting lips
Soft caresses guiding hips

Do I believe in love at first sight?
Fighting desires with all of your might
The need of another drives you insane
The warmth of togetherness falls like rain

Do I believe in love at first sight?
Strong hands holding on tight
When body temperatures rise up
Yearning overflows a cup

Do I believe in love at first sight?
When I wade in thoughts of you at night
When lust takes the place of a forest scene
And you begin all of my dreams

Do I believe in love at first sight?
Like a beautiful song that soothes the night;
Life offers no greater surprise
Than falling in love before your eyes

Kidnapped

I kidnapped you at midnight
Amid my desperate rage
I trapped you in my fairy tale
Unwilling to turn the page

I offered you my passion
I hid from you my lust
I devoured your opinions
I denied you my trust

When morning found us
Embracing without rage
I gently kissed your lips
And released you from my cage

Beyond Not Seeing

I would like to be honest with you
My inner being, my inner self
About your life within your health

I would like to understand your ways
Why you roam through endless days
On broken promises of a long-ago craze

When winter chills only hold
Memories frozen from the cold
Searching for a place that has collapsed
Destined for a hold beyond your grasp

My inner self, my inner being
Try to see beyond not seeing

Reflection 2:
Poetic Interlude

Gamble

I would have bet my lucky penny
That nothing in this world could make us lose what we had
Looking back now, it all seems sad

I got so wrapped up in the mellow talk
The sweet talk, the slow, warm comfort of our pillow talk
I wore out my traveling shoes
Now I understand why the wise say alone a mile is a long damn walk

I would have bet my arrowhead nickel
That the sun was gonna shine on us a long damn time
We played in it, laid in it, and damn near stayed in it
Looking back now, I was half out my mind

I probably would have bet my 1964 dime
That the sweetness and meekness that brought us our completeness
Was gonna reign forever that final day; after never
Looking back now, I don't think it could ever

Now if over I could start, be more wise than smart
I would have sixteen cents and not a scratch on my heart

For Your Sake

Did you come here to make me frown?
To wipe the smile from my face?
Do you want to take my strength?
To fill your empty space?

Are you real or are you fake?
Someone that I imagined by mistake?
Should I give or let you take?
Just for the sake of you having

Shoulder

When you cried,
I tried not to cry
I wanted to be your strength

As I comforted you,
Your sorrow
Became mine

I found it hard
Not to let your pain
Consume me

When your tears fell,
Resting gently
On my shoulder,

My skin
Bore the heat
Of your letting go

My thoughts lay damp
From the weight of your tears
Landing on my heart

Seven Days

Monday
The day you went away
My heart ached in a lonely kind of way
The clock ticked, yet held fast to time
As you ran circles around my mind

Tuesday
Found me longing still
For the dreams of you, my night had willed
Sadness found its way out
It toyed and roamed aimlessly about
Yet my heart kept clinging to a place
Still warm from your embrace

Wednesday
Rained with sleepy tears
Hiding quietly from what love fears
Pulling my heart string by string
Still allowing me to hear you sing
I watched as dusk began to fall
Willing you to call

Thursday
Came before I knew
Just how much I was missing you
It brought to me a wish to see
Beautiful you, holding me
A touch of wind blew through my hair
As night touched down its glare

Friday
Peeked through the window of my heart
Painting you like priceless art
Showing me a tempting fate
Making love; sit back and wait

Saturday
I longed to tell
Just how deep my heart fell
I had no sight or sound of you
No written words to hold onto
In my heart you had stowed away
Lingering yet another day

Sunday
Found me in a chill
Longing for your presence still
The silence rang loud in my ears
Escaping my heart as desperate tears

Cheater

It was my first night out with the girls ever
My man was out doing whatever
Even though it was never right

He walked in wearing that Casanova smile,
Claiming he enjoyed being out with the boys for a while;
Boasting was always his style

I began to feel awkward to blame
About a night that might have been the same
Had I stayed home

So, I sat, grinning and bearing it;
Smiling, 'cause my dignity required me to wear it

He tells me he is too tired to make love tonight
I smile, once more pretending that it's all right
Knowing that someone else enjoyed his sex

Lost

When I woke up this morning
And you were not by my side,
A part of me slept late

When I sat down for breakfast
And you were not there to pass the milk,
I drank my coffee black

When I watched the news this morning,
I shouted to you a forecast of twenty degrees
When you did not answer me, I left without my coat

Bouncing Ball

Shape me into a ball
Roll my thoughts away forever
Bounce me until I spin in the depths of confusion
Throw me until I land in a puddle of muddy water
But I beg of you;
Please don't drop me,
For my heart is not rubber

A Jolly Soul Mate

Waiting and wandering in
search of my soul mate
Discovering him in a season
That love has found too late

Pondering our lives meeting
Granting love a chance
Together our hearts are beating
Though forbidden from romance

Ticking clocks show time
Winding with windy fate
Ringing chimes still rhyme
To tunes of love found too late

Love echoes a whisper
Into waiting, wanting ears
In the voice of my soul mate
Love arrived too late to hear

Dear Friend

If ever I keep struggling for a love I cannot keep,
I want you to be the one to wake me from my sleep

If I ever find a love that you know will never pay,
I want you to be the one to help me find my way

If ever I find a love that you know will never provide,
I want you to be the one to help me decide

If ever I keep struggling for a love I cannot keep,
Please, dear friend, wake me from my sleep

Together Only in Love

Many lonely days have passed
Yet, love still occupies our hearts at the same time
We look at each other and ponder love
Knowing that together forever is out of reach
Gentle words escape our lips,
Entering our ears as whispered memories
An ugly reminder
Of what can never be beautiful as one
Long nights address our loneliness
As we sit in the same room far apart
Unwilling to chance our fate
We witness love wandering off, shaken and alone
Mornings interrupt dreams of one another
As we face our partners' happy eyes
We smile in spite of settling for those not our true soul mates
Wishful thinking weighs heavy on love
In the wake of our souls' yearning

Our hearts turn cheeks to ignore the pain of a love being strangled
Although our souls are true mates
Forbidden from enduring the sunlight
We love amidst the heartland
We hide together, loving desperately
We lie apart, dreaming of together forever

Runaway Love

It burns like a fire out of control
It travels like stone from a mountain; it rolls

It whirls like the wind on a blustery day
It fogs the eyes with a dust of gray

It shakes and wakes all from sleep
It steals from a heart what it longs to keep

It rakes a soul with claws of steel
It turns nightmares into something real

Memory

Midnight finds me steering clear
Of memories fond, yet seldom near
Portraits of a time once known
Now find me crying all alone

Morning sun comes without dew
Awakening memories of a grayish blue
Sprinkling drops of acid rain
As a memory stirs from the depths of pain

Afternoon brings without sleep
Reminders of a yesterday I long to keep
Evening finds me drifting through
A lost-and-found memory of you

Choices

Realizing that compromising
Is denying me the chance
To answer deep desires
That I long for in romance

All the hoping and the coping
With what's real and in my face
Gives some reason to believe
It was worth the short embrace

For the nights that I ignored warnings
Swept them quickly away
For each there comes a morning
When they must face the day

All the moving and the grooving
Just to keep in stride
Has me choking on my wishes
And throwing up my pride

Yet, my life is but a vehicle
That I have chosen to ride

Love Poem

I would like to write a poem
A poem about love
There would be no rhyme
No reasons
No sweet songs
Short goodbyes
Tears and more tears
A few broken hearts
Plenty of broken promises
I would like to write a poem
A poem about love
But I don't want to discourage anyone from finding it
It needs to be found
So that it can stop running from heart to heart
In search of its home

Half Past

The first time you tiptoed into my life,
Awakening me at half past midnight,
You brought me sweetness and warmth

The second time you tiptoed into my life,
Awakening me at half past midnight,
You brought me passion, lust, and the scent of romance

The last time you tiptoed into my life,
Awakening me at half past midnight,
You tiptoed away with my heart.
I have been dreaming of you ever since

Reflection 3:
Poetic Reckoning

Could You

Could you say that justice had been done?
If they put thirty-seven bullets in your son,
Could you sit and watch the news at night,
Knowing that your son was murdered in broad daylight?

Could you understand how a law-abiding man
Died with a wallet, not a gun, in his hand?
Could you look at the accused without hate in spite of your sorrow,
Knowing that your son was robbed of his tomorrows?

Could you hold your head up high after doing the best you could?
You raised a young man, taught him respect, yet where is the good?
Could you live with the jury's not-guilty verdict
Though it came with no solution?
Could you forgive the men who performed your son's execution?

COULD YOU?

Black America

This is America
Welcome to it
We the children
Must live through it

We must skip the alcohol
Ignore the dope
For we, the children,
Are the only hope

The burden is ours
At an early age
We must push forward
Swallow our rage

Walk courageously ahead
Acknowledging our past
while honoring the dead
Break the mold from which we are cast

This is America
welcome to it
We the children
Must live through it

Poetic Feelings

We must take the future
By its throat;
Wear our heritage
Like a coat

Take pride in the culture
We are derived from;
Conquer the vultures,
For they are sure to come

Climb to success at a rapid pace;
Keep our darkness close at hand;
Wear our strength upon our face;
Stay black in America's land

Suicidal Me

Look, world, can't you see?
I'm all messed up from trying
To stop myself from dying

I'm reaching out to thee
Can't you recognize a plea?

The world has made me tired
Must I quit before I'm fired?

Must I jump off a roof,
Fall dead on the ground,
Before you realize my body is falling down?

I am screaming loud and clear
My life is filled with fear

I am reaching out to thee
Please save suicidal me

World Gone Crazy

We mothers know
The world has gone crazy
Our grieving shows
Our dreams have become lazy

Our fathers see
Futures that are grim
From realities that be
Chances have become slim

We sisters demand
A sliver of choice
A unity
Within our voice

My brothers struggle to remain strong
While fighting to right another wrong
A simple act of their souls trying
To stop their purpose from dying

We children cry out into the wind
To conquer hate with love and peace
To let the vicious dying end
Let the devils' fighting cease

I Am No More

She beat against the brick wall
Until blood covered her tiny fists with anguish
She cried tears that rolled down her face like rain
And turned into the corners of her slightly opened month
Her body fell limp against the cold and dirty cement
Giving way to another loss
One that just might claim her weeping soul
She whispered, "No more, no more. I am no more."

She lay beside her dead son
The streets had already claimed two of her children as its own
Now the only child that she had left lay dead before her
"No more, no more. I am no more."
With her arms wrapped around him,
She lay still in a pool of her son's blood
And died in a puddle of her own tears
She is no more

Don't Judge Me

Stop. Don't judge me
It is not your place to begrudge me
Always hyping and stereotyping
You don't know my name
Always shelling blame
My life ain't no game

I have walked down many dark streets
My heart thumping to a different beat
My soul rose from the heat
I won't stop; I can't accept defeat

I have had hunger pains come down on me like rain.
I have witnessed death while trying to maintain
I continued fighting the strain for my gain
So, don't look at me with shame

Country rats lost in the naked city
The cost of life is the highest kitty
Pretending to be blind to the nitty-gritty
Straighten your lip and save the pity

For someone who wants to hear that flak
Not a soul like mine that has rounded the track
On my knees and on my back
Still, I refuse your offer. I will not crack

I managed to hold onto the rope
I swallowed some pride and choked on hope
I am here today because I coped

So, don't call me a waste
With your bitter words spewed with haste
When you ain't never had a taste
Of the ghetto life, the ghetto street
The life ain't rosy; the smell ain't sweet

What washes away uptown in a flood
Is simply dirt that's turned to mud
In the ghetto it's real; it's red; it's blood

STOP. DON'T JUDGE ME.

Trading Places

Let us consider trading places
We can start by trading races
I will be bright
Hell, let's call it what it is: I will be White
Let us take the deck and add a stack
You can be Black
Let's start with the shopping mall
We can call it a not-so-free-for-all
We can check out the boutique shop
We will enter together, but only you get stopped
I will walk around touching everything in sight
The salesman will follow you around and ask, "Sir, is everything all right?"
How does that make you feel? The White man came to shop;
The Black man came to steal. Shit just got real
My white brother from another mother
It hits different when you are the darker brother, and your blanket is no longer a cover
In our game of trading places, I like to think of it as trading races
An onus that cannot be erased, for you now have a Black face
I woke up this morning to a new beginning; I woke up White. I felt like I was winning
You woke up across the track, thankful you didn't die last night because you're Black

I want you to see my view from where you are
Tonight we drive each other's cars
Let's see how well you do; remember that you are me and I am you
You can drive my Mercedes; I will drive your Subaru
I am driving through the suburbs alone, cruising at 50 in a 25-mile zone

I blow past a cop on my right; I look in the rear-view mirror. No flashing lights
You, my Black brother, are doing 20 in a 25-mile zone in the suburbs one block from your home
You pass a cop on your right. Look in the rear-view mirror; damn flashing lights
You wonder if you will make it home because you are Black and you are alone
Let us consider trading places
We can start by trading races

Resistance/Existence

I am tired of the struggle
Tired of seeing dark-skinned bodies lie like rubble
It is plain for all to see
How America decimates me

The death toll grows wide and vast
Bleeding brightly before the mast
Reminiscent of the past

If eyes were created to see
How can the world be blind to me
A transparent reality that all mankind is not free

America continues to feed the racist breed
While allowing them to shoot my people dead

A dignified man kneels on the ground
Upon his head a peaceful crown
A silent protest abounds

If we stand, we stand for this
How do we fight and still resist
A justifiable homicide list?
The death certificate reads "died trying to exist"

If society does not blend,
The ill-acknowledged cycle will not end
A dying breed cannot mend
On a hanging tree that does not bend

It is a time long-ago defined
Where innocence becomes a criminal without crime

Is America the great
Just a place where people hate?
Is it a land not rendered free
For people reminiscent of me?

I hear many voices among the chatter
I hear people say all lives matter
The sudden sound of gunfire causes all to scatter
Yet it is only the blood of my people that is splattered

Hand to Hand

If we could get our priorities straight,
Maybe our black race could relate
To like thy neighbor, love one another;
Stop the killing of our dark brothers

Keep our sisters on their feet;
Teach our children not to be weak
Stop the violence; stop the hating
Band together and start participating
In life

Find out what you lack
Teach our children to be proud to be black
Thirst for knowledge; feed the mind
Let them know black is not a crime
It is a color

We are a strong race,
Tired of being disgraced
We are speaking up and stepping out of the category
We been striving and driving too long for our glory

We have been stopped before
We have been held back
We have had more than boulders in our tracks

We have been chained and even caged
All we fought with was our rage
It was the only weapon that we had
Until it started turning our race mad
The time has come to stop and ponder
How to keep our race from going under
Too many lessons rendered naught
From unnecessary wars that we have fought
And lost

Let us be the college
That feeds our children knowledge
 Let them learn what we had to live
Show them blackness does not have to give in

To those who try to hold us back,
We the African ancestry known to them as Black,
In the past we were forced to twist and bend;
We only took what they refused to lend

A simple chance to prevail,
To keep our brothers out of jail
Instead of a life of crime and facing hard times
An equal opportunity could direct the mind

Poetic Feelings

Forward, straight ahead
We don't want to read about them being dead
I don't want to see my sisters bleed no more
When a chance is all they are jonesing for

We are trying to teach our children to be strong
When every day they read that Black is wrong
We have to stop waiting around, be a part of what's going down
We have fought too long to go back underground

We have accomplished so much, come too far
To take another lashing, wear another scar
The time has come for us to stand
Black to Black, hand to hand
God is a colorless man

Take Me, Africa

Twenty-eight years I have survived this forsaken land
From the small of a child to the large of my maturity
For years I have wondered why my fit does not fit in
Why my eyes see sights of a far-off land
Why my ears pound with the sounds of a conga
Why my mouth hums to music which I do not understand
Take me back twenty-eight years before my introduction
Birth me at home in Mother Africa
Let my culture soothe the soul that cries for her
Take me back
Take me home
Take me, Africa

Young Guns

A teenager with a problem speaks
in a voice unheard by most
A teenager with a gun
Speaks in a voice we hear.
A tone that we recognize
We do not hear the clicking of his confusion
Yet we recognize the clicking of his young gun
A teenager seeks to survive
We do not pave a way
When a gun is fired,
Two roads are immediately paved
One to death, the other prison
Listen carefully to the clicks
Hear the young man
Before the young gun

Reflection 4:
Poetic Fortitude

Mother, May I?

Mother, may I talk to you?
I now understand what you have been through
I am walking the road you walked alone
I am moving boulders and turning over stones

Mother, how I envy you
My road ahead is long and cluttered
Through the storm my heart has uttered
You did not start your days not trying
You did not end your nights by crying

Mother, may I talk to you?
I have tried to do what you have done
I have fought my battles one by one
I have searched for the answers to my troubles
I found them deep within the rubble
I have learned to live with my mistakes
I have learned to give what life must take

Mother, how I envy you
I know the battle you fought for years
While taking on the world in spite of your fears
I now understand why you danced alone
In the living room of our childhood home

Mother, may I talk to you?
I want you to know that I will make it through
I will break the cycle you asked me to
I will cherish your courage and all of its pain
My life, like yours, will not be lived in vain

Mother, how I envy you

Note: I Slipped

I fell down hard today
It seems somehow, I lost my way
My heart stopped beating; though badly bruised,
My emotions took flight and began to peruse

I gathered my thoughts and repacked my load
As I gazed ahead at the dark, damp road
With fear in my heart and tears in my eyes,
I summoned my strength and began a slow rise

While searching to find a grasp for my grip
I made note: it was not a fall; it was a slip

Carry on, Sisters

It's the latitude and the attitude minus the gratitude
That has us searching for some solitude
It's the nitty-gritty of the self-pity
That has us hiding out in the dirty city
It's the prying, the lying, and the nonstop crying
That has us struggling to keep trying
It's the love sparing and the man sharing
That has us fighting mad and swearing
It's all the taking and the shaking from our hearts breaking
That has us making plans of escaping
It's the taunting and the haunting from our souls wanting
That leaves our anger flaunting
It's the gripping and the hyping from the painful stereotyping
That leaves our eyes sore from wiping
It's all the lusting and the busting from fool-hearted trusting
That has left our emotions rusting
It's all the commanding and demanding without the understanding
That has left our souls no landing
It's all the scoping and the hoping for the doors to finally open
That leaves us barely coping
It's all the wrong that has gone on for too damn long
That has our sisters struggling to carry on

Shoulder

When you cried,
I tried not to cry
I wanted to be your strength

As I comforted you,
Your sorrow
Became mine

I found it hard
Not to let your pain
Consume me

When your tears fell,
Resting gently
On my shoulders,

My skin
Bore the heat
Of your letting go

My thoughts lay damp
From your tears
Landing on my heart

It Ain't Easy

Walking alone ain't easy
Most of the time it's hard
Seems life has stacked the deck against me
And I don't have no holding card

Living alone ain't easy
Most of the time I'm lost
I just keep right on giving
When I don't even know the cost

Sleeping alone ain't easy
Most of the time I'm scared
Seems I'm always giving
To those who never cared

Crying alone ain't easy
Most of the time I'm sad
Dreaming is even harder
When it's for something
You never had

My Dues

I have borne a child
So, I have given birth
I have traveled enough roads
To belong to the earth

I have gone to school
For thousands of days
I have learned enough
To go my own ways

I have been quiet
So that I could one day speak
My mind has been strong
When my body was weak

I have been blind
So that I could one day see
I have also been caged
With hopes to be free

I have seen enough birds
To belong to the fleet
I have paid enough dues
I have earned a receipt

Cleanse Me

Wash the dirt from my body
Guilt has splashed on me
Rid my mind of muddy waters
Life has let me see

The filth of failure
I have waded in
The dust of maturity
That has settled on my skin

The lint of embarrassment
That has controlled my mind
The musk of greed
I have smelled in my lifetime

My Birth

On the dawn of my birth,
Were you assembling lyrics to sing
In praise of a new life?

Or were you left tearful
By the loss of a young girl's freedom,
Whisked away by the sound
Of my young soul crying?

On the eve of our first meeting,
Were you still attached to my heart beating?
Or was I a drum silently falling
On deaf ears?

On the dawn of my birth,
Were you comforted by the warmth of my body
Still attached to you?

Or had you let go of me
Seconds before you held me?

One of Us

There must have been a reason
Why things ended up this way
Maybe we were too optimistic
In doubting a final day

One of us had to be the revolutionist
One of us had to fight the war
One of us had to find the intuition
That was not there before

One of us had to turn and walk away from a complicated situation
One of us has to go on to seek a final destination
Two paths have been made for us to go them alone
To clear our paths of troubled stones

We must try to live up to our own expectations
Making our way through life's complications
One of us had to find the strength to write the final chapter
Just as one of us will lie disillusioned the morning after

One of us had to fight the temptation of letting our feelings grow
One of us had to fight the existence and let the other know
But I never thought that the one of us would be me
Who let my devotion take a fall and somehow stumble free

In His Hands

I went to God with my life
I placed it in his hands
I had no requests
God gave me no demands

I waited rather impatiently,
Afraid of the outcome
I spoke to God more frequently
I was beginning to trust him some

God did not badger me
For the things I had done
God only comforted me,
Easing my urge to run

There were days when I cried out
I could no longer hold it in
I raised my voice to God in shout,
God cuddled me again

On many nights as I lay awake
God witnessed my heart weep
I sobbed and revealed my soul to God
As I drifted in and out of sleep

At times I could not speak to God
My words came without sound
Through my tears, God understood
God never let me down

Sistergirl

Tell them tall tales, sistergirl
When they come to rock your world,
When they reach to touch your hand,
Make sure they understand!
This is a woman's world, sistergirl

When they speak of selfish thirst,
Let them know just who drinks first
When they try to bang your drum,
Let them know from where you have come
It's your world, sistergirl

Let your strength speak first, not last
A wisdom from days gone, not past
When they come to rock your world,
Tell them tall tales, sistergirl

Any Other Road

I wonder how many times I have cried
How many times I have tried to walk away

My feet just won't carry me down any other road
Except the one that I'm on

I wonder how many blues I have sung
How many shirts I have wrung
My tears out of for love

I wonder how long it would take
To separate the tears from the years
Way too long when they all came together anyway

Sometimes I get so bored of lying to myself
And so damn tired of crying to myself
But my feet just won't carry me down any other road
Except the one I'm on

95

It appeared that I had arrived at another dead end
So, I stopped and put myself in park
I adjusted my seat belt, lit a smoke, and shifted my mind into gear
I took a good long look at my route to nowhere

I decided right then and there to turn off my pipe dreams
I clicked on my high beams, folded that doggone useless map
I changed my route from nowhere to somewhere else

I was heading down the road of opportunity with what was left of me
I went through my knapsack, grabbed my jeans, my boots, and my cap
Burned what was left
I let those sad memories roll off my chest

Placed myself in drive and headed down 95
Looking for a place to arrive

About the Author

C L Jones is from upstate New York.
I began writing at the age of 10.
Writing about my life experiences and my love for survivors.
I believe that every stone has a story.
Every path is a journey, and all souls are worth loving.

My Dedication

*The book is dedicated to my strength
and my weakness—*

*My children Fred and Kelly.
My heroes.*

www.ingramcontent.com/pod-product-compliance
Lightning Source LLC
LaVergne TN
LVHW041650060526
838200LV00040B/1781